DEATH-BED

CONFESSIONS

OF THE LATE

COUNTESS OF GUERNSEY,

TO

LADY ANNE HAMILTON,

DEVELOPING A SERIES OF MYSTERIOUS TRANSAC-
TIONS CONNECTED WITH THE MOST ILLUSTRI-
OUS PERSONAGES IN THE KINGDOM.

To which are added,

THE QUEEN'S LAST LETTER TO THE KING,

Written a few days before her majesty's death,

AND OTHER

AUTHENTIC DOCUMENTS,

NEVER BEFORE PUBLISHED.

I am the viper that has been secretly wounding you both.
Vide the Countess's Narrative.

LONDON:

1822.

ADVERTISEMENT.

THE interest attached to those mysterious transactions, which involved the life
of an illustrious female in the most trying
difficulties, which caused her to roam, an
exile from the land in which she should have
enjoyed regal dignities, and that, ultimate-
ly, broke her noble heart, and laid her in
a premature grave, has not yet passed
away. The more they are developed,
their importance must increase; and the
more that truth is hidden for a time, like
persecuted virtue, the more glorious will

be its splendour and its triumph, when suffered to emerge from the clouds that enveloped it. The declarations of the death-bed are generally allowed to possess veracity;—it is then that pomp and ambition lose their power; and it is in the solemn moments of approaching fate, that the conscience-stricken mind attempts to make some feeble amends for the load of injuries it has heaped upon the head of the innocent.

Among the number of those individuals, who appear to have voluntarily contributed to embitter the life of the late royal victim, was, according to her own acknowledgment, the late countess of GUERNSEY. On her death-bed, this lady drew up a narrative of the share she had bore in the intrigues which were attended with such fatal results; and it will be admitted, on perusal, that none of the publications, which

have yet appeared, relative to the causes
of the queen's sufferings, have thrown so
much light on those mysterious transactions as the following "Confessions" of
the penitent countess, who was herself a
companion and attendant of the illustrious
female she confesses to have betrayed.

The narrative is written with fidelity
and minuteness, and strikingly evinces the
power of conscience to inflict an awful retribution for guilt, even on the minds of
those who revel amidst the luxuries of a
court, and are blessed with the most envied gifts of fortune.

say; but we feel assured that, to the mind of the attentive reader, no circumstance can possibly operate against the *authenticity* and genuineness of the following "CONFESSIONS." We shall, therefore, briefly observe, that the substance of them is most decidedly correct, having been communicated by the party to whom alone these facts were disclosed by the dying countess. It was her last wish that they should be made known to the illustrious lady concerned; and their truth, and the melancholy event of their arriving too late at Brandenburg House for the purposes of justice, and, perhaps, for the arresting the progress of the royal victim's fatal malady, are matters quite notorious in that circle, wherein alone they have as yet transpired.* It would be well DID THEY ADMIT

---

*Although the party who has entrusted the manuscript to our care has permitted us to make

OF CONTRADICTION; but while the reader
is earnestly assured that it is only from a
matter of delicacy that parties and authori-
ties are not more explicitly named, the edi-
tor has to regret that he can challenge,
with a sigh, THE REFUTATION OF A SINGLE
FACT contained in the "CONFESSIONS" of
the unamiable and unfortunate countess of
Guernsey.

Deeply, however, as it is to be regretted that the developement of the crafty
and mysterious transactions detailed in
these "CONFESSIONS" did not take place
earlier, yet it must be highly gratifying to
every lover of truth and justice, truly con-

known the *cause* that prevented its being delivered at Brandenburg House in time, we decline doing so, feeling assured that, though it might gratify
idle curiosity, there is *now* no necessity for in-
volving a single individual in trouble, which an
exposure of that circumstance would, in all probability, be the means of.

solatory to those who cherish the memory
of HER whose noble soul sought refuge
from a world of wo in the mansions of
heaven, and the delight of every Briton
whose heart beats with love for his sovereign, that these " Confessions" tend to
place *the real character and conduct of two
most illustrious personages* in a far more
amiable point of view than the fiends of
party would desire; for they will not fail
to perceive that the basest passions that
ever influence the human breast were in
constant action to excite in noble minds
unjust suspicion and malignant jealousy;
and to mar the happiness of two beings of
the most exalted rank and the highest at-
tainments, who were bound by every tie,
human and divine, to be the solace and
delight of each other.

CONFESSIONS, &c.

HONOURABLE LADY ANNE HAMILTON.

IN my retirement from a world which I have seen enough of to despise, I feel an anxious desire to repair the injury I did to a certain exalted lady, and know no better mode to disclose my sentiments to your ladyship, who, as the friend of slandered innocence, will, I am sure, find a pleasure in reading the following true, but humiliating statement.

This will be delivered to your hands by Mr. S——, but not till after my death. Pity my errors, and publish them only so far as may be necessary for the peace of her whom I have so deeply injured! Tell

her she is amply avenged, and that m
tortured soul has often envied her cal
enjoyment.   *   *   *   *
    *   *   *   *   *

It is now useless, dear lady Anne, t
speak of those youthful days when the ne
glect of every thing serious, and the pur
suit of frivolous amusements, laid th
foundation of a life of misery; but a
when you read this, it will be to you a
the voice of my departed spirit, (for alas
I feel that my tide of life is ebbing,) I wil
acknowledge, that, bending before the
shrine of vanity, flattery was my greates
enemy—the one before which every good
resolution yielded;—yet, surely, to lov
the prince must have been a pardonabl
offence! he who was ever so engaging, s
handsome, so irresistible! he who, at th
time of which I speak, was blooming i
the vigour of manhood, extolled by hi
own sex, admired, I might say adored, b
our's;—who would not have felt prou
when distinguished by his favoured atten

tion? My heart beat high when he retired
from the adulation of the court, to recruit
his spirits in a lively conversation with
me, and was pleased to call those his hap-
piest moments! Who would not have
dreaded a rival in such a bosom? My lord
Guernsey loved him, and was himself
pleased with his selection of me as his
friend; his royal mother insisted on my
filling a place in the family circle; and
said George was dull whenever indisposi-
tion, or other unavoidable circumstances,
caused my absence. Yet it was in this
high society I learned to be artful, and
that I became an adept in the science of
intrigue. I joined with the young ones
in deceiving the king, who was averse to
every expensive pleasure, and delighted
in the quiet and innocent employments of
domestic life. I have been informed, that
during the first fifteen years after his marriage, he spent the hours he could spare
from business in reading to the queen;
improving her in the English language,

and all things fitting her station; and, by way of a temporary relaxation, I know that he occasionally employed himself in the exercise of some mechanical work. His majesty never missed an opportunity of conversing with men from whom he had any probability of gaining information respecting the general state of society, with a view to any benefit that might be derived by the country over which he presided from such communication. The evening diversions were music and cards, the latter was admitted to prevent the queen's *ennui*. As the children grew up, these innocent recreations were declined by degrees; a musical party was always formed, which usually ceased at ten o'clock, or soon after; it being his majesty's constant practice to rise before six, on which account he quitted the family circle early; the queen usually left the room with him, but soon returned. The young people then began to enjoy their ease; for, with the exception of A—— and her

youngest brother, who were very attentive
to their father, the others were reserved
in his presence. Though the old gentleman encouraged their confidence, by his
good humour and willingness to enter into
their youthful sallies, his kind-heartedness
received a continual check, so that he became sensible of it; and, seeing they considered his presence a restraint on their
cheerfulness, he no longer enjoyed the society of his family, but retired earlier, and,
when with them, was less talkative than
formerly.

At that time I was young, and too
much engaged in the amusements around
me to regret the king's absence; I speak
of the year 1787. About that period we
lost, for a short time, the ornament of our
society—the all-accomplished and graceful prince of Wales: conjectures were
vague and various; some said "the prince
had taken an excursion to the coast, having accompanied a friend on his return to
France." I felt not a little proud that I

had been admitted a party to the secret of
his being gone to take a peep at Paris; but
this the Parisians were not intended to
know, his object being just to look at their
then beautiful queen, and to play one game
with her at *rouleaux*, under the incognito
of an English nobleman; as, also, to satisfy
himself whether the fashionable Made-
moiselle de Salle was as pleasing as Fanny:
and to try the affections of the facinating
widow Fitzherbert, who was then in Paris,
and about whom his head had wandered
ever since he met her at her uncle's. His
absence did not exceed fifteen days;* his
return home was hailed, by his mother
and young friends, as a joyful event;—to
me, however, it became less so, when I
heard that the widow had returned with

* This minute recapitulation of events, many of
them of a nature somewhat trivial for the purposes of what may be called a death-bed letter,
will not appear out of character, or extraordinary,
to those who knew the singular habits and mode
of thinking that always characterised the writer.

him. At first, I endeavoured to think it
a mere flirtation—an ephemeral passion,
for well I knew the susceptibility of his
heart! and, as long as I enjoyed his friendship, feared not the flatterers of a day!
But rumour soon told a tale which the
prince did not contradict even to me,
"That Mrs. Fitzherbert met him at
Calais, where they were united according to the forms of the Romish
church." The relatives of the lady whispered this every where; while the prince's
intimates pledged themselves to negative
the fact. Meantime, two houses at Brigh-
ton were fitted up in an accommodating
style, so as to admit an intercourse by a
private passage. The lady assumed a
great degree of stately *hauteur*, refusing
access to many of her former acquaintance, and all within her mansion bore the
mark of royalty. No one acknowledged,
yet every one treated, Mrs. Fitzherbert as
consort to the prince, and their domestic
happiness was the general topic, which,

however, I was little inclined to credit, the prince being equally ardent in his pleasurable pursuits, and equally warm in our private interviews! That he lived with the lady on a different footing to the usual style of a mistress was apparent; and the circumstance being related to his father, the latter was so hurt at the statement that it materially affected his spirits. The bare suspicion (for he never ascertained the matter satisfactorily) that his son should have acted contrary to the laws of succession, so preyed upon his mind, that, with other family disturbances, it produced a violent paroxysm of a disorder which was near proving fatal to his life.

Mrs. Fitzherbert continued the serious friend of the prince, and was gratified to the extent of her wishes. Pride being her prevailing passion, appearances were, to her, every thing; the soft emotions of the heart she was ever a stranger to. The queen noticed her, as did several of the family; the old lady pretended to believe that Mrs. Fitzherbert kept steady the affections of her favourite son—but here she tied a bandage over her eyes, from a wish not to see.

The state of society was then very gay. Mrs. H—t, a leader of fashionable diversions, opened her house to the great world:—here, the beautiful duchess of D—— shone unrivalled; the lovely Mrs. D—ff, with the lively duchess of St. Albans, the prince, with his fair friend, Fitzherbert, and S——; in short, all the distinguished characters of the day played their various parts: and masked assemblies, so favourable to the lovers of intrigue, were frequented by all the beau-monde. After sharing the delights of this *coterie*, though not always with unalloyed pleasure, I usually finished the day at the palace.

In the then state of things the king began to feel uneasiness regarding the succession: the pleasing expectations in which he indulged at the union of his second son had vanished, on hearing that

Frederick was as regular in his visits to
Mrs. C——y as before his marriage; the
good old gentleman remonstrated with
him on the subject, bringing forward (in
the way of example) his own conduct with
regard to lady Charlotte L——, towards
whom he had felt a great attachment,
founded on her amiable qualities, and
which he effectually conquered. The ex-
postulation was heard, but not heeded.
In 1794 his majesty was convinced that
the duke lived in a state of separation
from his wife, though not on grounds of
personal discord; the duchess being truly
amiable in manners, but afflicted with ner-
vous complaints, which rendered any
hopes of a family fruitless;—no wonder,
then, that the king should feel anxious to
see his eldest son settled: to this step,
also, the first minister was a strenuous adviser—and the parliament, being urged at
that time to pay the prince's debts, made
it a condition that he should take a wife.

This was a measure that made me determine on a plan at which I now shudder.

The story of the prince's marriage with Mrs. Fitzherbert had gained universal credit, notwithstanding the assertions of his friends to the contrary: Pitt, a staunch protestant, dreaded the influence possessed by Mrs. Fitzherbert, it being well understood they lived in great domestic comfort; and though she had never proved *enceinte* by either of her former husbands, and that the present alliance was null in every point of law, yet the birth of a child would have been regarded as an event likely to produce very fatal consequences; particularly as at that time, (doubtless to please Mrs. Fitzherbert) the prince showed a strong partiality towards the body of Catholics, even so as to raise their hopes to the attainment of emancipation at no distant period. This apprehension being exaggerated by the ministers in their statement to the king, he resolved to make any

sacrifice to prevent it. In the early part
of that year, he had repeated interviews
with the prince respecting his marriage
with some royal foreigner, the interests of
whose family might assimilate with his
own in religion and general politics. Not
but that the king felt delicately for Mrs.
Fitzherbert's situation; and both he and
the queen honoured her with their private
approbation; at the same time he could
not conscientiously, countenance so con-
spicuous an example in his son, as the
living in open violation of the laws, which
it was no less his interest than his duty to
practise and defend.

Never had I thought the prince so cap-
tivating, as at the moment when he informed me of his determination to com-
ply with the request. " My debts will
be paid," said his royal highness, " and I
shall please my father." " Who," I asked, " is to be the happy lady?"—" That
is of little consequence," he replied; " I
hope she will not be so unreasonable as

to expect me to love her!"—" She will have a RIGHT to *love* you," I exclaimed; " THAT, *alone*, is sufficient to make any woman happy!" " One thing I am resolved upon," said the prince, " not to wed my mother's neice; because, knowing it will be out of my power to pay her more attention than outward appearance may require, I will not wound the queen's feelings by slighting her relative; nor will I subject myself to be teased into hatred towards one, who, if she act wisely, will have a just claim to my respect and esteem. A neice on my father's side will suit me better, for he, being much engaged with state affairs, will have fewer opportunities for observation, as well as less time to listen to the retailers of scandal."

I then begged I might have the honour of attending the lady, as it would give me, I said, the means of sometimes adding to the comfort of both. I certainly did not, at that time, contemplate the dreadful con-

sequences which might happen, but I felt
that my motive had much of selfishness in
it, as I knew that, by such occupation, I
should have it in my power to direct, in
some degree, their affections. We talked
much of the bride elect. Frederick had
seen his cousin, during a visit he made at
her father's court, and reported her manners to be extremely engaging, her disposition lively, and that the uncommon
ingenuousness of her heart laid her most
secret thoughts open to every observer.
" She will be quite an exotic here," he
continued; " now, she is the artless child
of nature; but when she has studied our
code of etiquette, under the direction of a
clever Englishwoman, she will become
one of our brightest ornaments; for she
possesses much good sense, which now
floats on the surface of an unsullied mind."
Here I interrupted Frederick's eulogium,
to observe, that " I had always understood the court of Brunswick to be the
most free and licentious of any on the

continent." "With justice it is so considered," replied the duke, " but her mother has taken care to keep her daughter uncontaminated by bad example! and, indeed, a volatile disposition, such as Caroline's, is too much engaged by the variety of its own ideas, to rest long on exterior objects. Her mornings are employed in study; her evenings in the society and amusements of young persons of her own age; and I cannot help thinking the mind is more innocently occupied when playing at *hunt the slipper* or *forfeits*, than in listening to the scandal of teatable chat, or attending to the cold formalities of the people, whose looks, while complimenting each other, convey to an intelligent mind, that their hearts are corroded with envy, malice, and all kinds of uncharitableness." Oh! thought I, we shall have lectures on behaviour from this paragon of moral perfection; but, as I hope to have a good deal of the management, I shall take care her *naivete* does not su-

persede that courtly spirit, which by keeping us in outward order, gives us a cloak
to private indulgence.

 Whenever I had any grand object to
attain, it was my constant practice to ap-
ply at the fountain-head; so that morning
I took my work to the queen's apartment,
for she loved to see us industrious, and
having told her majesty I did not feel very
well, and came to crave her permission to
pass an hour there, as her conversation
always operated as a cordial to my spirits,
I was most graciously ordered to be seat-
ed.   At first, I kept to common topics;
until, by degrees, I arrived, through a
winding path, to the comforts of matri-
mony; and, finding the theme not unpleasant, I said, " English wives are indebted
to your majesty for their felicity; your domestic happiness has become fashionable;
long may it please God to spare us the
example! for much I fear, the loss of your
majesty would not only be severely felt by
us whose personal knowledge has taught

us to revere and love you with filial affection, but our children would experience
the most woful effects from a change, and
morality itself would totter to its foundation." You do not surely suppose my
son would countenance vice?" her majesty eagerly inquired. "Too well I know
the prince's bosom is the seat of virtue!"
I as eagerly replied; "but to give a great
and general example, it is not merely necessary that a king should practice goodness himself, much depends upon his consort; experience has lately shown us how
little the former can effect, without the
concurrence of the latter. Who could
practice virtue more rigorously than the
late king of France? yet, the influence of
his unfortunate partner has proved the
proneness of human nature to copy vice—
and has evinced the great importance to a
state of mutual piety in the king and his
consort. One cannot contemplate, without shuddering, the dreadful consequences
of a licentious court; for such we must,

however unwillingly, acknowledge was the distinguished character of the infatuated followers of Marie Antoinette!"

"My dear lady *Guernsey*," said the queen, "to whom do you allude? you alarm my fears; the correctness of your ideas has gifted you with a foresight I am unacquainted with; I have often profited by your friendly and judicious hints; whisper your present apprehension——you shall not repent your confidence."

"Pardon me," I hesitatingly exclaimed, as I covered my eyes with my handkerchief, "my anxiety for the happiness of our beloved prince rendered me incautious; a dread lest his amiable disposition should meet one that is uncongenial in this expected union, led me to anticipate the fatal consequences which might result to future generations; and I have unburdened my thoughts where I ought to have concealed them." "Have you, then, heard any thing particular of the princess it is intended my son should es-

pouse?" asked her majesty. " Only, that
she is an exception to the usual manners
of the court in which she has been edu-
cated, and in which she is described to
shine as a paragon of perfection," I replied:
" this intelligence coming, too, from so
good a judge as your majesty's second
son, ought to have silenced every fear;
but my spirits are greatly depressed ; I am
unusually thoughtful to-day; whoever, like
myself, has experienced the happiness enjoyed by my family, in the condescending
affability of a queen, that is the admiration
of all Europe for her virtue and the chaste
manners of her court, must, naturally,
shrink at the remotest prospect of a change
—a change which I hope not to live to
see!"

" You, Lady *Guernsey*, of all the females
I have the pleasure to call my friends, are
the one I would, by choice, select, as the
adviser and directress of the princess on
her arrival in this country. Can you, do
you think, give up your time to this chari-

table purpose! Caroline's mother never was a favourite with me; she has her brother's failings, without his virtues, and is much too tame for her station. Could you believe that she has suffered the duke's mistresses to sit at her table? She writes, as an excuse, that she admitted them for peace sake, and never allowed her daughter's presence on those occasions:—it was purchasing peace much too dearly! she ought rather to have been turned out of doors than have allowed such scandalous proceedings."————A message from her daughter Elizabeth, who was very seriously indisposed, interrupted our *tete-a-tete;* but her majesty did not leave the room without having first obtained a promise, that, if the earl would consent, I should hold myself in readiness to attend on the expected stranger. I spoke of *maternal duties,* as the only impediment to my ready acquiescence in any measure which might in the least conduce to the happiness of any branch of her family. I guessed this sort of excuse would best prove my fitness for the office, as well as increase the queen's desire to engage me.

After quitting the royal presence, I felt not a little pleased at my prospect of acquiring, what, to me, was the most desirable thing in the world—to lead the affection of the princess of Wales in such a manner as to secure her husband for myself! To accomplish this, it was necessary I should deceive the lord of my bosom, which, from habit, was now become rather an easy task. Every one has a hobby, which, at times, his friends are glad to borrow. Lord *Guernsey* would have sacrificed all he possessed for the honour of being styled " friend to the king;" I had only, therefore, in this case, to place the words *benefit, advantage, honour, credit, popular opinion, loyalty* and *expediency,* in the best points of view to obtain my end; which I did so effectually, as to bring him to be exactly of my mind—a thing not very usual with married people.

In the month of December, lord M——
secured the treaty, by acting proxy for the
prince; and, in the beginning of 1795, a
squadron was prepared to conduct the
bride-elect to England. I excused myself from accompanying the expedition,
thinking it best to stay and receive the
queen's personal directions concerning
her new daughter—I also wished. to give
all the consolation in my power to the ex-
pectant bridegroom, with whom I had certain plans to arrange.

Mrs. Fitzherbert, the nation undertook
to sooth in the way most congenial to her
feelings—an addition to her income.—
From childhood, money and a certain
style of living, were the desired objects of
her choice; and she was happy in acquiring them, even beyond her sanguine expectation; inheriting from her father the
slender sum of one thousand pounds, she
depended on a delicate complexion, and a
pair of blue eyes, to do the rest. Vanity
found an entrance into the pious and re-

tired education of a convent, and her
school-fellows prophesied her longing
spirit would not rest until she acquired exalted rank. Without one iota of the tender passion, which, when felt in the extreme, forms excuses for a thousand fol-
lies, she became successively the wife of
two gentlemen of large fortunes, and of
respectable families; who, by their generous liberality, left her a handsome jointure,
that enabled her to support her rank in society; but, as the inclination to please did
not cease with the life of Mr. Fitzherbert,
she acquired the name of the *fascinating
widow*:—attracted by this distinction, the
prince wished to see her, and an appointment was made for the introduction to take
place at her uncle's; on that occasion she
speculated so far as to risk seven hundred
guineas on a lace train, which she had lined
with lilac, as the most becoming colour to
her complexion:—more fortunate than
many, her speculation answered! I shall
now leave this lady to enjoy her jointures

and annuity, her royal liveries and prince-
ly friends, as long as she can.

I did not, as your ladyship knows, proceed to Germany, but met the princess and
suite at Greenwich. Our first interview
took place at the governor's house. I certainly eyed her very narrowly, and thought
her highness paid more attention to commodore P———— than was quite necessary: she spoke English in the German
style, like the old queen, and her manners
seemed to me as far removed from courtly
rules as one can well imagine. I could
not find fault with her person—her face
contained some pleasing expression, but
it had too much of nature in it; she seemed not to take the trouble of disguising a
thought, or even of clothing it in the most
delicate garb, to be selected according to
the usage of every person of fashion—and I
exclaimed, mentally " how will the elegant
George receive this rude, unpolished piece
of sculpture !"

The thought instantly occurred to me, that I would pretend to mollify, in some degree, the disappointment he was doomed to receive; I therefore begged leave to withdraw soon after breakfast, under pretence of preparing for the princess; it being understood I had brought dresses from London, and wanted to point out which would be most proper. I then stole a few minutes to address the queen, informing her, " the stranger was deficient of those delicate attractions the prince knew so well how to select and to prize, and begged to assure her majesty, I took this method to acquaint the most amiable of men, that he must not rest on outward appearances, but give credit for the inward graces of the mind, which I hoped acquaintance would bring to light, in the female who had the honour to be selected as the partner of the prince, and to succeed (I hoped at a very distant period) the most revered and virtuous queen in the world!"

This note I sent off immediately, for I considered the importance of first impressions, and knew the intelligence would be communicated by the mother to her son, and would ensure that sort of reception for the stranger which I wished her to receive —and I had the pleasure to find, as I was present at the family introduction, that my plan succeeded. Certainly the king looked all satisfaction on that occasion; but a glance, transferred from the countenance of the princess to me, directed by the queen, accompanied with a raising of the shoulders, expressed her majesty's grief on the first interview, and the kind of sympathetic anticipation she felt for her beloved George.

My heart exulted in the general sneer I read on the faces of the girls, except Elizabeth, who had it not in her disposition to give pain to any human being. The bridegroom was the last to make his appearance in the family circle; and, spite of my endeavours, I was chagrined to per-

ceive more of tender pity than the disgust
which I had expected to see depicted on
his features. All eyes were fixed on the
prince, when, with more than his usual
elegance of manner, he bent towards the
stranger, and raised her hand to his lips.
I saw her eyes beam upon him, as on her
protector, to whom she was going to confide her future destinies:—the look pierced
my very soul; the fiend Revenge bounded
in my bosom—and I secretly vowed, that
no earthly power should rob me of the object I loved to distraction! and of whose
heart, until that moment, I never doubt-
ed myself to be the mistress. I dared not
fix my regards upon him; but, assuming a
smile quite foreign to my feelings, I tried
to attract the queen's attention, lest she
might also be inclined to compassionate
the being, on whom her son lavished his
kindhearted notice: her uncle felt too happy within himself to apprehend uneasiness
in any one, so that I had nought to fear
from his penetration. Besides the pleasure

of seeing his niece, the king had various
inquiries to make concerning his sister,
towards whom he preserved a strong affection. I was impatient for the conclusion
of this interview, which broke up to pre-
pare for the royal nuptials. I superintend-
ed the arrangements of the bride, who
really looked pleasing, even in *my* jaun-
diced eye. Determined to rob her features
of their happy expression, I dismissed the
attendants, under pretence of giving her
highness a respite for recollection, and
availed myself of the leisure moments to
add rouge to her before highly coloured
cheek; for it was the natural look of ease
and health that she possessed, of which I
aimed to deprive her. As I made this unbecoming addition, I observed to her,
" that Mrs. Fitzherbert was fair, and the
prince always wished her not to be sparing
of rouge:" she eagerly asked " Who is
Mrs. Fitzherbert?" I hesitated, looked
foolish, and begged her to excuse my in-
advertency, in having mentioned one whose

name I ought particularly to have avoided;
and declared, the interest I felt to render
her appearance as lovely as possible, had
made me forgetful of other matters;—she
persisted to inquire, and I to make excuses; urged at length by her entreaties,
I knelt before her, and, with convulsive
sobs, that I could well assume, besought
her not to name my offence to the prince,
who would never forgive my incautious
conduct, in speaking of a person who, certainly, *had seemed to share his affections*,
but whom there was no longer any cause
to suspect; she having consented to remain
retired and unnoticed. " Does any engagement bind the prince to that lady?" asked
the princess. " Excuse me," I replied,
" that I cannot answer that question now
—on some future day I promise to disclose
all." " On your honour, promise!" said
the princess. " Solemnly I do!" was my
answer: " but your highness is disturbed
—I cannot forgive myself—let me entreat
your highness will take something to re-

cruit your spirits." "A little cyder will suffice," said the princess; "the voyage has made me thirsty." I rang—an attendant entered; I ordered some cyder, as also some brandy, and mixing some of the latter with some cyder, assured the princess it would prove particularly refreshing after her journey. No sooner had her highness swallowed the overpowering beverage, than a message was brought that the ceremony waited her appearance, and she hastened to join the family who had assembled in the closet.

Never shall I forgive myself the mortification I had prepared for her—even at that time my heart reproached me, when I saw her bold and unbecoming manner, as she tottered towards her uncle. He, good man! fancied it was girlish agitation, whilst every other person beheld, with astonishment, the dauntless expression of her eye: fired with secret anger, and strengthened by the potent draught which the demon of mischief had impelled me to

administer—no timid fears caused a re-
tiring glance; on the contrary, her look
penetrated every countenance—but I alone
could read her thoughts! I saw that her
mind was absorbed in elucidating the
doubtful secret, and that she was employed
in seeking the object of her emotion in
every face. Unconscious of her actions,
and forgetful even of the approaching ceremony, until reminded, the procession
had formed for entering the royal chapel.
The duke of Clarence having led her to
her seat, the prince came next, looking
manly, handsome, and graceful. When
each person had taken his allotted place,
the marriage ceremony commenced; the
bridegroom's agitation was apparent to
all; he was so little himself, that he arose
too soon, which occasioned a pause, but
the king whispered something to his son,
who resumed his kneeling posture. Possibly no one could better account for this
absence of thought than myself: I saw him
look aghast when he first perceived his

consort's altered and strange appearance,
and pleased myself, as he gave the bridal
kiss, to think, how he would revolt from
lips that my arts had so recently sullied!

That night, the marchioness of T——,
lady C——n, lady C——, and myself, attended the princess to her chamber: I saw
her anxiety to question me, which their
presence prevented; she certainly did not
exhibit any pleasing expectation when we
took our leave. On passing the prince's
dressing-room, I met the faithful Troop,
carrying wine to his master; the man
shook his head significantly, as if to say,
" He should have done without this to
night;" whilst I mentally exclaimed, " I
envy them not, for well I know that few
approach the nuptial bed with less prospect of happiness!" Sure some evil spirit
directed me that day, or I could not have
devised so diabolical a plan; but my mind
was bent on the ruin of the princess, and,
after a night of inward agony, I arose with
new resolution to effect it.

Knowing the king's habit of rising early,
I walked before breakfast to B——m
house, and, going to the queen's apartment, tapped at the door: Sch——g opened it, and invited me in; I said, that, fearful
of not having an opportunity, during the
day, I came thus early, to inquire how her
majesty had borne the fatigue of yesterday.
"My good lady *Guernsey*," said the queen,
"this is kind; for heaven's sake tell me
what you think of the stranger? Mary
declares she never beheld such an awkward looking creature; and we all de-
plore the fate of our poor George; his father is the only person who seems blind
to the strangeness of her manner?" I dare
not utter my fears," I replied, "but, when
she has recovered the fatigue of her voyage, the princess will be more herself; she
will not then be troubled with *thirst*, as
she is at present." "I see," exclaimed
the queen, "really I thought she stagger-
ed at the altar.——How dreadfully shocking!
what had she taken?" "The princess in-

sisted on mixing brandy with her cyder," I replied; "indeed, she poured it
out herself, or I should have been more
careful." "This is monstrous! George
must be informed of her vile practice."
" Permit me to request your majesty's
forbearance, in this instance," I said,
" the like may never occur again," " promise," resumed the queen, " if it should,
that you will acquaint me." " I shall
conceive it my duty so to do," I answered, and excused my longer stay, under
pretext that the princess might want me.
On my return to Carlton house, all was
still in the anti-room. The criminal passion I had admitted in my bosom burned
within me, and I lamented having accept-
ed a situation which compelled me to witness the estrangement of the only heart I
had ever prized. Agitated with hope and
fear, as well as other stronger sensations,
I retired to a dressing-room, the door of
which stood half open, and threw myself
on a sofa, exclaiming, as I did so,

"George, I exist but in your presence; if my love must be sacrificed to this, coarse, untutored woman, I will yield my life also; since I could not live a single day chilled by your indifference." At that moment an arm encircled my waist. . . . .
Alarmed, lest it might be my lord *Guernsey*, and that he had heard my complaint, I was near fainting; when the most soothing accents lulled every fear: it was the prince himself—he closed the door and a conversation followed, the most interesting I had ever held. I gathered, in general terms, that I had nothing to fear from my rival; some half-uttered sentences implied disappointment, nay, a sentiment still stronger, disgust! Elated at the half-owned truth, my gratitude became unbounded as my love, and exulting in the confidence I had shared, I quitted the prince, to answer the bell which summoned me to attend his consort. I entered her apartment with a cheerful countenance, and ventured to inquire " if her royal high-

ness felt well and happy?" The princess
answered, with an air of lassitude, " I own
to you, my friend, I am not as comfortable as I expected." "Nature is very perverse," I observed, "for I can assure you,
every female envies your royal highness."
"I cannot see any reason;" replied the
princess. "Are you not the future queen
of England—allied to the best, most accomplished, and elegant of men!" The
princess, smiling, answered, "I am not
yet sufficiently acquainted with the prince
to pronounce him the best—I will give
him credit for all the manners and accom-
plishments which a man can possess; but,
with regard to *make*, or *form*, as you call
it, I have known many as elegant, or more
so; there is Mr. M——, for example, to
go no further." Now, in these observations, as experience has since analyzed
them, there was nothing improper; the
smile was good-humoured, and void of
any lurking ill; yet, did my prejudiced
mind give it a diabolical meaning; and, at

that moment, I resolved to twist and use
each word as might hereafter answer my
maddened purpose. Soon as breakfast was
over, I attended the bride to Windsor, and
a second and a third night had the mortification to see the prince retire to her chamber. No longer able to endure this appearance of harmony, I depended on my influence with the prince to procure a separation
of beds; so, on the morning, when we were
about to return to London, I contrived to
meet the prince in his dressing-room. I had
purposely taken off my rouge, and, with an
air of langour, which was partly affected
and partly real, I approached his royal
highness, to inform him of my intention
to remain a short time at Windsor. " I
gave myself credit," said I, " for a greater
portion of fortitude than I possess; I cannot endure to be an eye-witness of your
royal highness' happiness with one so
every way unworthy her exaltation; had
the princess been as amiable as you are
deserving, I hope, and believe, I could

have witnessed your highness, felicity, if not with pleasure—with patient forbearance—but, now, it is painful, in the extreme, to perceive so much worth and goodness lavished on a person who, by nature, is insensible to the blessing." "I think, with you, she is cold;" replied the prince. "No, no!" I observed, "NOT COLD; where inclination leads, she can be lavish of her love!" "I conjure you, by the friendship that has existed so long between us?" said the prince, "by that passion with which you have inspired me! say all you know—conceal nothing from me." "Pardon me, your royal highness, and impute it to my sincere affection, that I have penetrated so deep into the recesses of her heart. I may err in thinking as I do, and, for the future, will be more cautious in unbosoming my thoughts; I will no more dwell on words, but will wait until facts shall warrant my speech." "*Guernsey*," said the prince, "I believe you love me—not to think it, would be

worse than death, so entirely am I yours!
and I tell you, there is nothing in Caroline
to excite affection—her actions, and her
manner, are unfeminine; her language
coarse, and her whole person needs the
aid of English habits to render it even
agreeable . . . . and, much I fear, it will
never acquire the style of fascination,
which alone has charms for me! Never-
theless, as a stranger, she claims my protection; and I have been considering how
I can best fulfil the engagement I have entered into, without enslaving myself; for,
though the chain that binds us has not
been assumed from choice, I feel, as she
has been selected for my partner, and will
one day fill the station of queen of these
realms, that much is due to her from the
nation and from myself. The people
show every disposition to perform their
part, and I am no less willing to make
some sacrifices to perform mine;—I am
only puzzled so to act, as to render Caroline comfortable, without infringing too

E

largely on my own pleasures; outward appearances must be respected: now you, my lovely friend! can assist me in these arrangements; and first, we will devise a plan by which our mutual intercourse may be secured."

Piqued at the considerate manner in which the prince had spoken of his consort, in the first moment of irritation, I made this rash reply:—"To please each party, I beg your highness's permission that I may remain in this retirement, where, in the attendance on your excellent mother, I shall run no risk of hearing your name traduced by unfavourable comparisons with any man; painful as your absence will be, it will not be accompanied by the bitter regret of seeing your love abused."

"Have I a rival in Caroline's affections?" asked the prince.

"Surely, I have not betrayed the princess!" said I, fearfully.

"You have done only a part of your duty, said the prince," "and I trust you need no stronger motive than *my love* to complete the work, by naming the person who has dared to supersede me in her affections."

My refusal, dear lady Anne, was vain; so, after a struggle, which the eloquence of love overpowered, I related her words: "That she had *known* several more elegant in form than his royal highness, particularly Mr. M." and I took care to lay such emphasis on the word *known*, as should leave on his mind the strongest and most unfavourable impression.

"Enough!" said the enraged prince, "I swear to renounce, from this hour, all further intimacy with one so hardened in vice, so depraved by habit."

I became alarmed for the consequences I might draw upon *myself;* I soothed, solicited, and, on my knees, besought his forgiveness; protesting my sorrow for having repeated what my love, perhaps, had exaggerated into criminality. At length I obtained his promise that, for my sake, he would bury the cause of his conduct within his own breast:—this he pledged his honour to observe, and I firmly believe he has maintained his word inviolate.—With regard to his future behaviour, the prince was equally determined to confine his attention to outward form, saying, " She shall reside under the same roof, and share my protection and civility, so long as she acts in a manner to deserve them."

On our return to Carlton house, the newly-married pair maintained a sort of cool politeness towards each other. At the hour of rest they retired, as usual, to their dressing-rooms. When the bride had undressed, the prince led her within the door of her chamber; then, saying he felt indisposed, he kissed her hand, and wished her " Good night." I watched the countenance of each: that of the prince evinced a delicate kind of sorrow; the princess was evidently mortified—her pride dictated acquiescence; she returned

the wish without a question or a word of
complaint. When the same ceremony
had been frequently repeated, the princess,
one night, observed to me, that English
husbands had very singular notions. "It
is much the practice on the continent,"
said her royal highness, "for married people to have separate beds, and a very plea-
sant custom I think it is; but then their
sleeping-rooms join; here, I find, the husband sleeps at a distance: at least, I suppose so, as I have not received a nightly
visit since the third evening of our marriage."

"It is well known," said I, "among
the prince's friends, that he never passed
a night with Mrs. Fitzherbert: their private intercourse was not confined to time,
but was at the call of inclination; the best
mode, I think, to keep the flame of love
alive." "Apropos, *Guernsey,*" said the
princess, "you promised me some particulars respecting that lady; I wish you
would now communicate them." "I shall

obey your highness, commands," I replied,
"but hope to be excused the relation now;
for it is a long story, and my lord might
wonder at my delay." "Your apology
is so good," said the princess, "I accept
it with pleasure. I would not, for a moment, be the cause of disappointment to
you and your lord's happiness; therefore,
good night." As she uttered the last sen-
tence, her highness sighed heavily, and
looked so sad, that it brought reproach to
my mind. O! how would her wish have
changed, had the princess known it was
the prince who waited for me!

This reflection damped the pleasure
with which I usually went to his apartment; then, my heart was capable of com-
passion,—it has since become as callous
as flint. Had I, at that time, followed its
dictates, the anguish of this moment would
have been spared me! the bitter acknowledgment that I was the first to envenom
the prince's mind with base, malignant
stories, false as they were diabolical, that

I acted the part of a spy over his inclinations, to keep under, and turn aside, the
tide of his feelings, as they floated on his
naturally kind and well-intentioned heart;
that I so imposed upon his goodness, as
to convert his disposition, which, in its
original source, was benevolent and hu-
mane, into * * * * * * * * All this
haunts my guilty soul, and makes me odi-
ous to myself; but the deed is done! His
character * * * * * * * * * and
she, who was gifted with the means of
diffusing happiness around her, is a persecuted, suffering mortal! and what am I?
. . . . I dare not pursue inquiry,
lest madness seize the little memory that
remains, and so deprive me of the only re-
paration in a guilty wretch's power—to
own this was *my* work!!! * * * The separate beds at Charlton house, as soon as the
circumstance was known, became a subject of uneasiness to the king; he expos-
tulated with his son, who entered no farther into the matter, than to assure his

father it was mutually agreeable to himself
and his consort; and the old gentleman
learning, soon after, that his daughter and
niece was in that state in which "all wives
wish to be, who love their lords," con-
tented himself with merely advising his
son against indulging with other females,
concluding, that after the *accouchement*, all
would return to the right system. In one
part of his father's injunction I perfectly
coincided; and, to prevent the prince's
ranging in the sweets of variety, I kept
him as much as possible to myself; but
here I did not always succeed: his visits
to Mrs. Fitzherbert were more frequent
than I judged necessary; but, as his delicacy made him still consider it right to
continue his clandestine attention to her,
it appeared a fit occasion for me to communicate the nature of the prince's engagement in that quarter; which I took an
opportunity of doing, under a promise, on
the part of the princess, never to divulge
that the communication was made by me.

I declared my motive to be entirely devoted to her highness; but that if the
prince knew it, I should be considered, by
him, as a spy upon his actions; in that
case, I should be required to resign my
greatest happiness—the being allowed to
attend upon her person; in which pleasing
duty, I hoped to have sometimes the opportunity of evincing my sincere and
grateful attachment to her royal highness.
In relating the narrative, I took care to inform the princess, that *her* marriage was
not a voluntary act on the part of the
prince, but a task imposed upon him by
the people, who were instigated to make
this condition through the apprehension of
the ministers, who hoped, by this means,
to wean him from his catholic connexions;
for they looked with dread on the partiality the prince professed towards that
class, through his attachment to Mrs. Fitzherbert, who followed the Romish doctrine, in strict conformity to its tenets,
keeping in her house a chaplain of her own

persuasion, who was often admitted in the social circle of the prince.

The princess received the intelligence with an hauteur of spirit for which she was remarkable, and which gave her the appearance, to those not well acquainted with her, of want of feeling; but which rather proceeded from that greatness of soul that for centuries had characterized the Brunswick race. From that period Mrs. Fitzherbert was frequently the subject of our discourse, when we were together.

The prince continued to notice his consort; but even the ceremony of doing so was performed in a careless manner,—more as a duty he owed the public than out of any desire to oblige his wife. An incident, which occurred that autumn, increased his coolness, and confirmed the queen her implacable enemy.

It happened, that the Rev. Mr. Randolph had business at Berlin, and waited on the princess, to ask if she would honour him

with any commands. The princess, thinking this an excellent opportunity to send
to her father's court, had a personal interview with Mr. Randolph, when she requested him to deliver a packet into the
hands of her mother, and particularized
other commissions, all which he promised
to execute punctually. Mrs. Randolph
was then at Bath, in a delicate state of
health; as soon as her husband had left
her, the disorder took an alarming turn,
her life was in imminent danger, and an
express was hurried after her husband,
which reached him on the coast, just as
he was about to embark. It may be easily
conceived that Mr. Randolph's thoughts
were absorbed in his wife's situation.
Anxious to behold again the object of his
affection, he determined to relinquish his
intended journey, and to retrace his steps,
with all possible speed, to Bath; but, even
at that moment, the packet intrusted to
him by the princess was a principal object
of his care; and, to prevent the possibility

of giving that lady uneasiness, he went
through London, for the purpose of call-
ing at Carlton house. It happened, however, on his arrival there, that her royal
highness was absent from town: he enclosed the packet, therefore, and directed
it " *to the particular care of the lady in
waiting upon the princess of Wales,*" and
left it, with a strong injunction, to the
porter, that it might be forwarded next
morning. *I* was the lady in waiting; and
finding, on taking off the cover, that it
contained a parcel for the duchess of
Brunswick, I informed the queen; and, an-
ticipating how far her curiosity might lead,
when urged by my insinuations, I showed
the packet, remarking, at the same time,
" it might contain a journal, by its size."
Her majesty asked if the princess kept a
journal? I said, " it was her highness' custom to write her daily observations." The
packet lay upon the table;—its superscription, " *to be given to the duchess of
Brunswick, from her daughter,*" was a

strong inducement. " Doubtless," observed the queen, as she took up the parcel; " an insight into this would set all our opinions right."

" It would enable us to deal justly towards EVERY BODY," I replied, " and seems to be put purposely in the way. I do suppose it a duty, on the part of your majesty, to ascertain the truth; and, certainly, an occasion, such as Providence has here provided, may not happen again."

" Open it!" said the queen. Never did I obey any command with so much alacrity, and my joy seemed complete, when I perceived several pages of the journal which I had been in the habit of seeing the princess write. It began with her entrance on board the royal yacht, and was written in bad French, mixed with some English phrases. To any unprejudiced person, this packet would have afforded real amusement—the style was sensible, lively, and interspersed with

F

many ingenious sallies of the writer, who
expressed, with great justness, her con-
ception of the English character; and, on
the whole, conveyed a vein of satire, truly
entertaining. She described the manners
of the ladies, who were sent to conduct
her, with provoking accuracy; and spoke
of the polite attentions of the commodore
and the captain, in terms which I endeavoured to construe into more than mere
affability; assigning meanings that I well
knew were not intended. But the introduction to her husband's family was best
of all delineated; and some events of the
wedding-night were stated with admirable
talent, though with great good humour,
containing some particulars, told, indeed,
with delicacy, but which were only fit for
a mother's eye.

The queen, raising her hands, exclaimed, " I am shocked! what, my friend, can
be done for George." When the family
was described, the princess had drawn
each with such accuracy, that it was im-

possible to make a mistake. "To begin," said her royal highness, "with this unparalleled, virtuous family! among whom my good uncle is certainly misplaced, since he is benevolent, considerate, and virtuous, with a heart just like your own, so I shall put him up *on the shelf*, as the people here say, but not in their acceptation of the term, which implies one unfit for service; but, that he is beyond all comparison with them, I shall, therefore, pass on to my *snuffy* aunt."—"Monstrous!" exclaimed the queen, "me vow she is right wicked."

I own, I trembled for what might follow; and was almost sorry, when I found her satire attacked only the foibles of her husband's family, and would have passed, with well-intentioned persons, for mere playfulness; but we were not disposed to consider it in that light. Her majesty conceived herself grossly insulted, as though she had been accounted the worst of criminals. Elizabeth's taste for *fun and porter*, with Mary's *prying curiosity*, and for which her cousin styled her "*peeping Polly*," so roused her anger, that she seemed inclined to expose the whole to the prince; but the acme of her majesty's rage was reserved for the line in which the princess, describing the men's dress, on coming to the high collar, observed, " most fashions here originate in the convenience of the GREAT, to hide their *natural defects*." No longer able to bear, what she conceived to be an intended insult, the queen seized the packet, and hastened with it to the king.

Uncertain to what extent royal fury might go, I ventured after her; but I should need the genius of Hogarth to describe the scene which followed—I shall not, therefore, attempt it. Her majesty uttered her invectives in such bad English, and in so hurried a manner, that it was next to impossible to understand her; and the king was at a loss to guess the meaning of all this bustle, until, see-

ing the superscription of the packet, he
said, "Fie, fie, Charley! is this your
mode of protecting a stranger? what an
example do you set, in opening private
communications—read not another word—
but let *Guernsey* re-seal the packet, and
get her to make the best apology she can."
"I will keep it," returned the queen,
"that I may force her to confess her
shame." The storm now threatened on
the part of the king; so, seeing a contest
was about to ensue, I thought it prudent
to retire, and watch for her majesty, as she
passed to her own apartment.

Whilst waiting, I considered upon the
best mode of concluding this unfortunate
incident: and it appearing to me, that to
expose this packet to the prince would
cause a quarrel, and that her royal highness's present situation would immediately procure a reconciliation, I thought it
would better suit my plan not to allow the
discovery to be made; but rather to keep
the secret in reserve, since it might serve

the purpose of irritation, whenever I wanted something to rouse the prince's feelings; so, when her majesty returned, I curbed my impatience to speak, until I had first heard her opinion.

"The king," said her majesty, "with his usual perverse way of reasoning, has made me promise to return these papers, without seeming to know their contents; his silly fondness for his niece keeps him blind to her conduct, but I will find the way to punish her—I shall certainly perform *my duty*, in cautioning my son; and you, *Guernsey*, must contrive a way to enclose the letters as they were before— but how can we obtain the seal? for I see, that even in that, she has acted with her usual imprudence—would any other female, having the honour to be princess of Wales, seal a letter with a simple olive-branch? it shows the woman's meanness."

"I will answer for getting the identical seal," said I, "I am a prodigious favourite with Sander, and she will obtain it for me." I then retired with the packet, but before I closed it I copied all that related to the royal family.

From that day the family intercourse became less and less frequent; they met only when etiquette made it needful; and then the queen and her daughters (with the exception of Elizabeth) omitted no opportunity to mortify the princess's feelings: the latter affected not to understand their insinuations; she always appeared in high spirits, when in their company, and generally amused herself with asking the females to join her in a game at " hunt the slipper," or some other frivolous diversion, to which she knew they were averse, and at which she had, in fact, no wish to play herself, as she was then very near to her confinement; but her great spirits prompted her to sport with nature. Had she been fortunate enough to have had a good and gentle friend near her, to advise and counsel her against these playful sallies, it would have been well; but it was her mis-

fortune not to have such a friend. In many
points the princess was masculine; her
health and spirits were good, and being
naturally noble, frank, and generous, she
felt herself elevated by the approaching
prospect; for, although slighted at that
moment, she felt that she was about to
give birth to the future heir to all their
boasted power, and trusted to that epoch,
as the means of reconciling her in the
affections of her husband, and giving her
consequence in the eyes of his family and
the nation; and her spirits rose as she approached nearer the moment which was to
realize this fond expectation! This eleva-
tion of mind prevented her seeing the coolness of her husband's relatives; whilst
they considered her cheerfulness as proceeding from extreme thoughtlessness;
thus, deceived and deceiving, each regarded the other with a mortal indifference, which was daily growing into hate
in the one party, and disgust in the other.

Little apparent alteration took place,

until the birth of a daughter brought the
family arrangements to a sort of crisis.
This much-looked-for event was attended
with some unpropitious circumstances:—
that it was not a son, was a source of disappointment to the prince, but that being
a point which human foresight had neither
power to direct, or decide, he was induced
to bear it with tolerable patience—but,
that the birth should have occurred a day
sooner than the usual calculation admits,
was variously handled, according to the
interest, or accidental opinions of the persons who discussed it. The prince, who
is thought a good judge in some female
cases, silenced the kind gentlemen who
were disposed to advise, by saying, " he
did not wish them to trouble themselves
with the subject;" but his conduct evinced
a different opinion; for he ordered an additional private staircase to be erected,
leading to the nursery, by which means
he avoided the disagreeable dilemma of
sometimes meeting the child.

Notwithstanding the calumnious insinuations of the queen, who protested, "She should have been inconsolable, had such a suspicious circumstance happened to her," the princess seemed to have acquired a new claim on her husband, and I saw, with jealous malignity, that, in two months after the great event, he increased his attentions towards her; often, and I thought purposely made his visit at the hour he knew the infant would be present, in whose smiles he took a lively and parental interest. Fearful these appearances might lead to a reconciliation, I deemed it politic to re-peruse the contents of the packet, which had now lain a long time untouched. When, the next time, I met the prince alone, he asked me "What I thought of little Charlotte?" I replied, "I think her the most fortunate of children!"—"In what respect?" he asked.—"Because she has the most indulgent father and grandfather in the world," said I; and continued, "no one

can witness your increasing fondness,
without admiring your extreme kind-heartedness." "Who do you think her like?"
said the prince. "I conceive the child bears
some small resemblance to her mother," I
replied; "but few persons are inclined to
see that." "What is the general opinion?"
inquired the prince. "My regard for
your royal highness does not allow me to
repeat unpleasant things; therefore, I request your permission to change the subject." Here, as I expected, I was interrupted, and urged by the most endearing
entreaties, until, in half uttered sentences,
I conveyed more to the prince's mind
than an exposure of the packet could have
done; and took care, during the following
days, not to allow his royal highness leisure for reflection, as I met him, seeming-
ly by accident, when he retired from the
family circle. Knowing his heart was
well inclined to listen to his consort's ex-
culpation, I considered the interim, in
which his ideas wavered *pro* and *con*, a

most important crisis, and resolved to secure it my own. For this purpose, I held
counsel with the queen, whose mind was
more bent on the continued separation
than even mine.

We conversed on the negligence which,
for some time back, had been shown to Mrs.
Fitzherbert; and, thinking I should please
her majesty by forwarding a reconciliation
in that quarter, I represented her temporary absence, as the effect of delicacy giving place to public feeling, the better to answer my purpose. I pretended to have received a communication from lady M——
L——, who mentioned having a letter
from Mrs. Fitzherbert, from the other
side of the water, and in which she acknowledged the motive of her journey in
the following passage;—" I do, and ever
shall, consider myself the lawful wife of
the prince; I am convinced he thinks the
same, and that his excellent father and mother (whom all the world allow to be the
most pious and amiable that wear a regal

crown!) are of the same opinion. I am well
aware that the late marriage was in com-
pliance with the will of the nation; therefore, from a consideration of public benefit, which often operates against individual
interest, I will absent myself awhile, not
to be in the way of those feelings, which
must be sacrificed to female delicacy; as,
certainly, the exalted stranger will require
some time for explanation. When she
knows how each party is situated, doubtless, she will herself invite my return; well
satisfied with holding the prerogative of
royalty, whilst I enjoy the supreme felicity
of conjugal affection; mine, by the most
sacred tie! the duties of which shall never
intrude on the rights annexed to her high
station." . . . . "Who,"
said I, "can help admiring such sentiments! here, the most tender conscience
may see the forbearance, the noble feeling, by which a wife is enabled to resign
the outward appendages of rank, for the

G

mild and unobtruding practice of social duty."

With arguments such as these, I reconciled the queen's conscience with her inclinations—and with others, quite as convincing, to the prince, I succeeded in chasing the tender sentiments which had latterly lurked in his bosom for the princess. Though still living under the same roof, they seldom met; the habit of cold indifference they had hitherto carried towards each other had now grown into visible dislike, which the princess, from the ingenuousness natural to her disposition, first showed she had discovered.

That the prince and his royal partner had laid aside the wish to please each other, was apparent to every one;—that their forced interviews were accompanied with mutually painful sensations, was certain, to those who had the power of observing them. These reflections formed the ground of my excuse for counselling her majesty (who honoured me with her full confidence) to encourage her son in the renewal of his connexion with Mrs. Fitzherbert, and I prepared *his* mind to receive this advice, by frequently speaking to him on the subject, and describing the sensations of that lady, as I pretended they were stated by her friend; for to me she was not half so formidable a rival as the princess, because Mrs. Fitzherbert possessed not any share of that susceptibility which is irresistible when displayed to a man of feeling; but there was in the princess a noble frankness, which, united with greatness of soul, and a kindly nature, would have been all-powerful in its operation; and I was aware, if these qualities were allowed scope for action, they would, in time, excite the prince to more manly conduct, and plant in his bosom a mean opinion of the families, who had been, from childhood, his favoured companions.

* * * * * * * *

Here a weight of reproach preys on my

spirits for my guilty conduct at that period;
doubly guilty! from the false friendships
I assumed, as a cloak to my infamous de-
signs; for I now acknowledge, with sorrow, that I brought on an attempt at
explanation from the princess, who, mov-
ed by the most honourable sentiments,
frankly declared, that it was better for
married persons to separate formally, than
to meet only for the purpose of irritating
each other. This conduct, on her part,
was interpreted, by my insinuation, as proceeding from a sensual affection for those
rites, from the enjoyment of which she
had been so long debarred; and gave rise
to that memorable letter of the 30th of
April, 1796. I need not dwell on the result of that epistle; every one knows it
was followed by the dismissal of wife and
child. But every one does not know what
sacrifices this proceeding cost the parties.
The prince suffered the greatest uneasiness, which I endeavoured to tranquillize,
by fabricating scandalous stories about his

consort, and assuming increased tender-
ness towards his person; then, finding
these efforts insufficient, I had recourse to
a more powerful auxiliary, and induced
the queen to use her influence in bringing
back Mrs. Fitzherbert. The prince grew
ill: this did more than the most persuasive
arguments: the lady returned; and, with
her presence, the prince's peace came also.

During the term of nearly ten years,
did the princess stand the test of severe
scrutiny, before her enemies succeeded in
any serious cause of accusation. Many
were the battles I then fought with my
conscience; I often admired her magnan-
imity in so bravely meeting the repeated
injuries which succeeded each other as
quickly as the inventive genius of her enemies could create them.—It was the dread
I felt, lest her conduct should obtain a
reconciliation with her husband, that induced me to lend myself as the instigator
of what afterwards went by the name of

"The devil's plot." To this I was urged
by a confession made by the prince, ".that,
in a tipsy frolic, he had passed a night on
the Heath;—had slept in his consort's
chamber, and, in contradiction to the sentiments expressed by himself in 1796, had
infringed on his voluntary terms of per-
petual separation." On the credit of the
old adage, that drunken men and children
speak truth, I concluded this visit was one
of inclination; and when the prince owned
having made a promise to revisit the Heath,
I thought it right to use every means of
prevention. I began by rousing the fears
of his mother, who had immediate recourse to lord M——, whom her majesty
knew to be her son's confidential friend,
and the repository of all his secrets! in return for which honour, lord M—— sub-
mitted to lose his money, looking always
to an appointment in the East as an equi-
valent: this convenient compact bound
them friends; and the queen, wisely guessing that the cause of her son's aversion to

the princess had been imparted to his
friend, suggested to the latter the suspicions she had long entertained—and he,
comprehending the heinousness of deceiving majesty, engaged the brothers to prevent the prince's promised visit, by devis-
ing amusement elsewhere, that drew him
to a distance from the Heath.

Meanwhile inquiry was set on foot
among the princess's household, which,
by means of douceurs, proved pretty successful; for, from the epoch of the boy,
William Austin's admission into the family, lady Douglas and myself had made
him the groundwork of a plot, which it
was our intention to play off at a proper
opportunity. In this, I must confess, lady
Douglas was the complete dupe, at which
I felt no kind of sorrow, as I owed her a
grudge on an occasion which I shall here
mention.

When lady Douglas appeared, for the
first time, with a title at the drawing-room,
the prince, who never omitted an opportu-

nity to say a civil thing, paid some frivolous compliment on the valour of sir John,
at Acre, which she imagined was spoken
for the purpose of admiring her beauty.
Prepossessed with a notion that the prince
admired her, she, one day, in passing the
princess of Wales, curtsied with a sort of
impertinent sneer, that said, " I am a favourite." The princess, who was never
backward in penetrating the thoughts of
others, knew how to interpret this behaviour. " I see," said her royal highness,
as she was one day conversing with me,
" lady Douglas has a great inclination to
conceive herself of sufficient importance
to become my enemy; I will punish her
vanity by affecting to notice her friend, sir
Sidney, for I have discovered that she is
in love with him." " May it not turn out
a dangerous experiment?" I asked the
princess. " I shall know where to stop,"
her royal highness replied; and effectively
she lost no time in commencing her plan.
When she next dined at lady Douglas's

she paid the most marked civility to sir
Sidney. The princess called him to a
chair next her own, allowed him to serve
her with fruit, and, on quitting the house,
told sir John and his lady, she hoped they
would not visit her unaccompanied by
their friend; and afterwards sir Sidney
waited on the princess, at a general invita-
tion. The success of any playful frolic
always caused the princess to be in excellent spirits. I never observed her manner
so pleasantly cheerful as during the period
that sir Sidney made one of the dinner
circle, which happened at least twice in
the week. About this time William Austin became an inmate of the household;
prior to his arrival, lady Douglas had assumed an extreme affection for the princess, though to me, in whom she placed
confidence, she acknowledged herself an
enemy; and the malignant expression of
her countenance, whilst making the strongest protestations of regard, discovered to
such a keen observer as her royal highness

the deep-rooted hatred with which she
was endeavouring to probe the secrets of
her heart. The princess told me of it, and
that lady Douglas had introduced the subject of her and sir John's attachment to sir
Sidney, for the purpose of hearing in what
terms she would speak of the hero. "I
equalled her in cunning," said the princess; "I made her believe me to be in
love with him, and left her ready to burst
with spleen at the idea that he loves me to
desperation.—I will make her mad before
I have done with her, for I will dress
Sander, and give her the key of the shrub-
bery-gate. I saw lady Douglas look very
significantly when sir Sidney mentioned
his intention to stay some days in London—she fancies he will remain that time
concealed in this neighbourhood, for the
purpose of carrying on an improper intercourse with me. You know there is a
stranger (a poor deranged gentleman, they
say,) come to reside in the white cottage:
Sander shall enter the private gate from

that direction, wrapped in my travelling
cloak, and lady Douglas, whom I know
will be on the watch, will transform every
moving figure into sir Sidney, and will
think herself secure in stating my guilt.—
Should she dare so far, I will expose her
malice in telling the whole truth—the
scorpion of jealousy shall sting her to the
quick for her wicked dissimulation."

"This would, indeed, be excellent," I
observed, "could your royal highness be
certain of the sequel; but is it not possible
that calumny may succeed in spreading
her rumour to your injury, before your
royal highness has an opportunity to re-
fute her testimony?"

Entertain no fears on my account," said
the princess, "so well am I convinced of
lady Douglas's improper attachment for
sir Sidney, that I have it in my power to
make her retract, by a single word, spoken
in the hearing of sir John."

When things were in this state, I called
upon lady Douglas, and, having insinuat-

ed to her the princess's fondness for the gallant sailor, had the pleasure to hear her acknowledge, under the mask of a friendly intention, (very commonly assumed on such occasions,) that the princess had *almost* confessed her guilt. " I doubt not," continued her ladyship, " that, before sir Sidney's return, I shall be in full possession of the fact. I wish," she added, " that her royal highness would not make me her confidant; it will be the most distressing thing in the world, conscientious as I feel in my duty to my sovereign and his amiable family! you know it would be impossible for sir John to conceal such an important circumstance, and it would be doubly guilty in me, who am doatingly fond of my husband, to conceal secrets from him—of such a nature, too! it would be enough to give him a wrong opinion of me; I would not, for the universe, be suspected of an intimacy with a female of such a character."

" I took upon me," said I, " to assure

the princess of *your delicacy* on this subject, in a conversation she held with me
relating to sir John and his friend."

"Could she entertain any doubt?" has-
tily interrupted lady Douglas.

"On no surer ground," I replied, "than
that certain persons always imagine a very
intimate friend of a husband has favourable opportunities with his wife."

"If I could suppose the princess entertained so horrid an opinion of me," exclaimed lady Douglas, "her high rank
should not be any inducement for me to
continue her acquaintance; I would instantly relinquish it!"

I found but little difficulty in dissuading
her ladyship from a rupture at this crisis,
and things went on, apparently, as usual.

On sir Sidney's return to his friends on
the Heath, the whole party met at sir
John's table. The attachment between
the ladies appeared then to have reached
its height, each having an object in view;
the princess being desirous to mortify her

II

neighbour in the most vulnerable part—
her affection for sir Sidney; and lady Douglas was bent on the destruction of the
princess. In this humour the ladies met,
and then the memorable story of the milk
wetting her royal highness's handkerchief,
with the fabrication of her approaching
accouchment, were personally related by
the princess. Of this I do not entertain a
doubt, all the particulars having been told
me by lady Douglas, and afterwards confirmed by the princess herself, who, ignor-
ant of the imprudence she was commit-
ting, thought only of playing, what she
termed, a frolic.—I was the most guilty of
all; since, in order to punish lady Douglas's hypocrisy, I wrote the anonymous
letters to sir John, and enclosed the offensive caricatures, in which I copied the
princess's writing so exactly that it would
have been difficult for herself to have de-
tected the fact; these letters brought the
intrigue to an issue. Lady Douglas, irri-
tated to excess, repeated all that the prin-

cess had told her, to sir John; the latter
repeated it to the duke of Sussex; he con-
sulted his brother E——, and it was resolved to enter on a thorough investigation
of the whole matter, and make the result
known to the prince. I have reason to
think they were deterred, at that time, by
learning that the princess had played off
some trick on lady Douglas, which information I have always attributed to Sander,
as I believe she was the only one, except
myself, who was in her royal highness's secrets.—For me, I never divulged the truth
until now, that remorse extorts it from me.
For nearly two years this business remained unnoticed, only that E—— advised with
the princess respecting a more guarded
conduct in future, and that the affair was
whispered to each one in the family, with
the exception of George and his father:
but, in two years after that period, when
the husband's unexpected visit to the
Heath, roused the fears of the enemy, that
a reconciliation was to be apprehended, an

union of interests induced them to join in
a sort of family compact, to prevent the
frustration of their hopes; and, encouraged by the protestations of sir John and lady
Douglas, who offered to attest their depo-
sitions on oath, they laid the affair open to
the king and queen.

On that occasion, two of the brothers
took upon themselves the right of exam-
ining the cottage on the Heath, which had,
for some years, been the residence of a
character unknown; they went when the
owner was absent, and found in one of the
sitting-rooms an unfinished likeness of the
princess of Wales. This, at the time, appeared a mystery, that astounded the
finders of the portrait, but which no one
tried to penetrate. Her enemies considered it the most favourable occurrence that
could have happened; and, perfectly satisfied with this seeming proof of criminality,
immediately entered on the scrutiny I before mentioned; and a noble earl, who,
hitherto, had been considered amiable in

manners and disposition, meanly lent himself as the agent of persecution.

Her royal highness, on hearing that
doubts were entertained as to the proprie-
ty of her conduct, asked for an immediate
change of the persons who formed her
household, feeling it was incumbent on
her not to allow herself the possibility of
tampering with her dependants. Had she
behaved with equal prudence on all occasions, how admirably she would have acted! It was a remark of doctor Johnson,
" that persons of strong sense are apt to
perform the ordinary actions of life care-
lessly; whereas they encounter great events
with cautious prudence and wisdom."
Such was the case of her royal highness,
who stood on the rectitude of her actions
and intentions.

They whom the king appointed to investigate the business also acted conscientiously, and satisfied their master there was
no real cause for banishing his neice from
his presence; but, when the king's inten-

tion to appoint an early meeting was made known to his family, her enemies had recourse to their influence with the prince, and succeeded in prevailing with his royal highness to solicit a delay.

On the whole narrative being related to the prince, he declared that he could never regard as virtuous, a female who wished to appear guilty; and asked my opinion. I replied, " that no woman in her senses would have advanced such a falsity of herself; that either lady Douglas had fabricated the whole story, or that the princess, in a lively mood, had committed herself to her friend, and then made up the strange story she imparted to me; but," I observed, " I now speak only my natural sentiments, without the chance of guessing how a person, with feelings so opposite to those I entertain, would act." From that hour the prince's hatred became fixed; even when his counsel, after minute inquiry of each of her enemies, yet wanted proof, and, therefore, could not advise against the

princess being received in the family circle, he still remained unmoved,—determined not to sanction her reception, he
absented himself from that memorable interview. Meanwhile, the princess continued to act as she had done before, except
that she showed a great attachment to the
foundling William Austin, and an increased contempt for her husband's family
—the natural results of being debarred the
company of her daughter, and of being an
object of dislike to her deluded husband.

After remaining some years persecuted,
harassed and unhappy, the unfortunate
lady wrote one of the best letters she ever
penned to the prince, in which she stated
some of the many hardships she had en-
dured, and regretted, in feeling and res-
pectful language, the loss of her daughter's society. The minister, whose office
it was to read all letters to his royal master, observed, when he concluded this, and
had laid it aside, " that some mode must
be adopted to prevent the prince from

being troubled with these interruptions,
from one who ought to be satisfied with
the permission to retain her title and dignities." Nothing more was said at that
time: in a few days, however, a copy of
that letter found its way into the daily papers. An interested friend of the princess,
who was then treating with ministers for
an augmentation of salary, thinking it
might answer his purpose, procured the
original letter from the secretary's desk,
and made this malicious use of it. And
it did answer his purpose; since, on his
taking the paper to his patron, and assur-
ing him he furnished " the intelligence,"
he obtained the desired appointment, and
from that day, has been an active agent
against the princess. Meantime, the prince,
who was naturally kind, and possessed a
great portion of good sense, had often,
when alone, ruminated on the contents of
his consort's letter; the more he considered, the more he became convinced of the
reasonableness of the arguments it con-

tained; and had actually debated the matter in his mind, by arraigning the merits
of the case before him, and had come to
the determination of making some personal inquiries, whether things were, really,
as bad as they were represented. This
was the subject of his royal highness's me-
ditation, when the same officious adviser,
who had read the original letter, appeared
with the offensive publication in his hand,
which put all disposition to justice to
flight, and fanned the smothered embers of
revenge into a flame, which all the force of
pity could not allay.

The man in office met that day his *con-*
freres at ——, and after dinner, amused
them with an account of the purloined letter. Exulting in their triumph over an un-
resisting victim, they agreed to form a
league with the lady's friends and advisers;
so, under the appearance of friendship,
they informed Mr. W——d, that nothing
would tend so effectually towards the princess regaining her husband's esteem, as

her making a tour to the continent; as, by
that means, she would leave her daughter
unbiassed with respect to marriage, and
free her from many restraints, resulting
from the coolness that now existed between her mother and the members of her
father's family, which coolness, they said,
would wear off by absence, and that, at
her royal highness's return, every thing
would be on a right footing.

As soon as this proposal was communicated to the princess of Wales, she entered, very willingly, into the plan, and
immediately made her intention known to
the ministers, requesting them to inform
the prince, who considered this step as a
fresh proof of his consort's depravity;—
rejoicing, however, that it would for a
time, at least, free the country from her
presence, he readily consented.

At that period, I was myself smarting
under humiliation, being convinced lady
Hamilton was my successful rival. Glad
to avail myself of a temporary change, I

seized a hint, thrown out by the prince
" that a person in France would have a
good opportunity of watching a certair
lady's conduct," to say, " I would make
a visit to some friends on the continent
from whence I should have it in my powei
to inform him of what was passing.'
Pleased with my offer, the prince repeatec
a rhapsody of affection, which my hear
inclined me to believe; but, thinking i
might not seem well in me, as her partj
were suspicious of me, that I should leave
England at the precise time she did, I em
ployed my confidential agent, madame
B——, and she placed Louisa Demont ir
the way of the princess, as a person qua
lified to answer the double purpose of ob
taining her royal highness's confidence
and betraying it.

I have reason to believe it was the prin
cess's intention to have remained only a
short time abroad, with her relatives ir
Germany; and that the " long journey,'
as it was afterwards called, was underta

ken in consequence of her finding the heads
of the continental courts in league with
* * * * * * against her. "This," exclaimed her royal highness, when one day
conversing on the subject with Louisa,
who obtained the situation of her dresser
" this is more than I was prepared to
meet; yet, this offensive and cruel conduct is the work of christian princes, who
preach religion to unenlightened nations,
and hold up charity to be a godlike virtue!
The heathen practices it better—he only
immolates to the presiding power, whom
he believes it to be his indispensable duty
to please; but christians sacrifice to every
passion that agitates the human frame. I
will devote myself to two years' absence;
surely, in that period, my consort's eyes
will be open to the conduct of those
wretches who have too long influenced
his weak sensibility. Some of my enemies have paid their debt to nature. Alas!"
she added, " I myself may have ceased to
be an object of persecution! these things

are wisely hidden from us. Be they as
they may, I will endeavour to gather
knowledge and patience by studying the
character and manners of those who live
at a distance:—perchance, I may meet
with hospitality where there is no profes-
sion of it."

" Where," asked the prying Louisa,
who had already ingratiated herself into
favour, " does your royal highness mean
to bend your course?"

" When I have seen the best part of
Italy," said the princess, " I will proceed
to Constantinople."

" Bless me!" exclaimed Louisa, " will
your royal highness venture among infidels?"

" Most certainly, it is my intention,"
continued her royal highness, " and if you,
Louisa, entertain any fears of the climate,
or that your beauty dreads a Seraglio, I
counsel you to go no farther than you
deem yourself safe—I have no fears on my
own account."

In the next letter, Louisa said she had
conquered her apprehensions, and was
determined to accompany her royal mistress. "Knowing the princess as you do,"
said my correspondent, "your ladyship
will not be surprised to hear, she has
made acquaintance with a courier, who
disentangled her train in the gallery at
B——, with a grace that charmed her ro-
mantic taste. Inquiries respecting the
hero were entered into, which ended satisfactorily: seeing I should anticipate her
royal highness's wishes, I mentioned him,
the other day, as a fit esquire for the long
journey. ' With your royal highness's
permission,' I said, ' such a gentleman
seems a very necessary part of the suite;
he has intrepidity to contend with Turkish
valour, and I know a secret, that would
remove every cause of scruple, respecting his admission to the honour of your
royal highness's society, *that his family is
more than respectable.'*—"Explain yourself," interrupted the princess. ' That it

was noble,' I replied, ' before certain va-
lorous deeds, in favour of Buonaparte, rendered the present descendant famed, 'tis
true, for courage, but degraded in the eye
of monarchy.—I heard Marto say, that he
was honoured and loved by men of all degrees.' The bait took—I have perceived
my mistress conversing with Bergami in
her out-door excursions, and not a few
weeks will place him high in her affection.
For my part, I wish we were all returned
safe to christian quarters, and wonder what
can induce the princess to wander among
those heathenish Turks. However, I shall
go, to prove my gratitude to your good
ladyship, and my willingness to serve the
cause of virtue; for, to be sure, as your
kind ladyship says, it must be serving her
to put trials in her way, so that, if I should
be sacrificed by the infidels, I shall fall, as
lord Nelson said, ' doing my duty.'

* * * * * * * *

Here was a chasm in our correspondence
until the year 1817, when I had another

letter, containing numerous instances of what Louisa termed the princess's mean disposition. How, from the moment of her setting out, she desired the persons of her suite to forget the difference of station; that each should exert himself for the amusement of the others, whilst she should endeavour to study the comfort of all, and share, equally, their pleasure and fatigue: " and, sure enough," said Louisa, " the princess kept her word; we were all as one family, and, except sometimes that we slept on straw, and had not sufficiency of what was good to satisfy our appetites, and that the plague was at our door, we were pretty comfortable; and I must own that the princess seemed as happy as any of us.—I thought it prudent, before we sailed for Turkey, to give my humble advice, that her royal highness would allow Bergami to act as her guard. I "have heard," said I, " that Turks are naturally treacherous, and that they always carry arms; should they," I continued, " be ever in-

duced to use them, (as heathens will do any thing for money,) your royal highness's attendants would not only suffer the most poignant grief, but might, at their return, be subject to injurious suspicions."
. . . . Thus was the princess induced to admit Bergami to *act* as her personal protector. In the next letter, from Como, Louisa informed me that things were no better than before the long journey—that the foreign ambassadors were equally uncivil, that the house of B——n, in particular, had given unequivocal marks of disrespect—besides, that the ministers at her own home couched their letters in very mysterious terms, and not at all conciliatory. She also mentioned, that her mistress frequently spoke of returning to England, but she hoped her royal highness knew better than to put herself in the way of being called to an account;—for, when two persons slept under the same tent, it was but natural to suppose they must sometimes meet;—in a

storm, for example, people think themselves safer for being near each other.—
An apprehension of something of this kind
prevented my placing my bed by that of
the princess, which her royal highness was
anxious for me to do. . . . . To
be sure, it may be said, that the awning,
not being fastened down, was liable to be
lifted up by any one; but, who would venture to look into the privacy of a princess!

This letter anticipated my anxious wish;
I showed it and talked over its contents
with the queen, lady Hamilton, and a few
particular friends. We all affected to la-
ment that a person, for whose connexions
we felt so strongly, should have so far degraded her friends. About that time, lord
M—— and his lady returned from the
continent, having been so shocked by reports concerning the princess of Wales,
that they said they had left Italy in disgust. They communicated their intelligence to the duke W——, and he, *out of
brotherly affection*, told it to the prince; the

latter, galled to find the honour of his
family so grossly impeached, and hoping,
he said, to contradict the report, ordered
certain persons to investigate the whole
affair. Accordingly, Mr. B——, being
a shrewd lawyer, competent to discrimi-
nate the nature of claims of right between
a client in disgrace and a powerful defend-
ant, was thought by the prince's friends a
proper man; and, to aid in the difficult
task, Mr. C—— went also; but, to conceal the motive, the latter received a sine-
cure office of ambassador to a court with
which, at that time, the English had no
communication, so that he had ample
leisure to make inquiry. At the end of a
few months, both gentlemen returned,
freighted with a cargo of intelligence sufficiently doubtful to create suspicion, and
short of facts to substantiate what they
advanced. Nothing gives such unlimited
latitude to opinion, as when the imagina-
tion is left to follow its own bias. In this
dangerous crisis of the business, I receiv-

ed an unexpected visit from the man of
law. No sooner was Mr. B—— announc-
ed, than my thoughts reverted to the princess, now styled queen; the prince of
Wales having succeeded to the august
station of his deceased father.

This was our first meeting for the space
of eleven years;—after mutual inquiries of
each other's health, about which we felt
mutually indifferent, Mr. B——, who con-
siders minutes lost that do not bring their
share of profits, preluded the business by
saying, " a late death had opened a field of
difficulty to our beloved sovereign. As
the adviser of his consort, and from a wish
to act rightly, I presume," said the gentleman, " to consult your ladyship, on the
present proceeding between his majesty
and the queen. You, madam, know the
king's unvaried desire to do justice to his
cousin; and you know, better than any
other person, what has been her conduct,
from her first arrival in this kingdom.—
Many criminating circumstances have

been proved by those who had access to the lady—all short of the fact of adultery, it is true—now, I will not be so rude as to quote Latin to your ladyship, but our law says..........."—" I understand you, sir," I observed, " and reason tells us, that the wish to commit a crime constitutes guilt."—" Doubtless it does, madam," continued Mr. B——, "the king's conscience tells him he ought to have the benefit of this indulgence; and they now have the subject under their serious consideration; still a *tender regard* for the lady renders them anxious not to advise to her injury, and desirous to act on a sure foundation. I, myself, have often shuddered at the consequences her conduct might draw upon her, when the question should be put respecting her filling the seat of the late strictly virtuous Charlotte. Yet, with all her excentricities, the queen has so much innocent playfulness in her manner, that often, during my late visit to her, I was tempted to suppose she was making dupes of us all. Sander, who, from long knowledge of her royal mistress, gave her tongue more freedom than any other person, once said, in my presence, 'my dear princess is the best creature in the world, and one would think she wants to appear the worst.'

"The confidante is no more. Your ladyship is now the only person in existence, to whom the princess's private intentions were fully known."

"I had rather not be questioned," said I, "for it would hurt me to turn her accuser."

"No one," said Mr. B——, "who is acquainted with the amiable lady *Guernsey*, could ask a thing so unpleasant to her nature—the favour I come to solicit of your ladyship (a favour in which the country is deeply interested) is, that you would inform us, to the best of your knowledge, whether, on the former trial, there were legal cause for the plea of adultery? I presume not, after the usual

form of law, to question you, madam, respecting time, place, or person; all those
matters may be easily supposed; only your
ladyship's opinion, as a highly valued
friend, whether the princess was, at that
time, guilty of adultery."

"If my answer is to be productive of
any consequence, affecting the queen's life,
I shall feel most reluctant to give my
thoughts utterance." "Your ladyship
need not speak more fully," the lawyer
replied, "nor shall I trouble you, madam,
further on this very unpleasant subject.
The consequence of your ladyship's com-
pliance will merely be, that we shall prevent
any further exposure. I must be plain in
telling your ladyship, that a legal trial
might be attended with very unpleasant
disclosures of family matters, and end in
punishing the guilty. The change in the
liturgy must, ere this, have made known
the public opinion; it shall be my business to caution the queen against returning

to this country; the state will provide generously for her comfort."

The lawyer having, as he thought, gained the purport of his errand, soon took his leave; whilst I endeavoured to believe that had he remained until morning, I should have made him acquainted with the whole truth, and have stated the princess's conduct in 1806, and also have shown him the letter forwarded to me from Philadelphia, in the latter end of 1807, which letter, to answer my own guilty purpose, I kept to myself, but which I shall now enclose as an additional proof of the queen's innocence. Mr. B—— allowed no time, thought I, for this act of justice; and when I considered what examination of events, long passed and forgotten, must have followed such a statement from me, and reflected on the consequence which must have resulted to myself, that my artful plans would have been laid open to the king, and my dishonour published to the world—and that a sort of conspiracy would thus have been acknowledged to have existed against the queen even prior to her landing, of which the royal family would appear as the instigators........these and similar reflections made me feel satisfied with the allusion I had given; had I acted differently, thought I, I might have brought the king's friends into a very awkward predicament; whereas, the present course will not endanger any one, nor injure the queen, since it is intended that she shall be rendered comfortable.

A few months intervened, when I met lord L⸺ at the house of a friend—he found an opportunity to thank me for the satisfactory intelligence which, through my means, he had received. "It has perfectly tranquillized me and my colleagues," said lord L⸺, "without the knowledge of your ladyship's opinion, whose uniform attachment to the family on the throne has stood a test, we might have been over cautious in giving our advice on the queen's unexpected appearance in this country; we were certainly tenacious of forming our opinion from interested reports, lest we might occasion irreparable injury to an exalted female, who naturally looks to the law for justice, and to its ministers for protection.—You, madam, have removed a weight from our minds, as we feel ourselves justified in advising the present mode of conduct, which nothing short of the basest depravity, in forcing her presence on her indulgent and amiable consort, could have induced his majesty to adopt. But there is a soothing balm to those, whose office obliges them to harsh measures, in knowing they are really acting with lenity; and we are wholly indebted to lady Guernsey for this valuable feeling."

From that day I have sustained an accumulation of mental and bodily afflictions.

The daily papers have been read to me, from which I have learned the whole mass of evidence for and against the queen, and the system of persecution which has been practised, seems to have all originated with me! Shame, attending the confession of my guilty deceptions, has, hitherto, deterred me from bringing forward a statement of the truth. I feel it my duty to say to his gracious majesty, supposing your ladyship will perform my last request of showing this letter to our sovereign—*" I am the viper that has been secretly wounding you* BOTH *for the last five-and-twenty years; I caused you to assume a cruelty of behaviour towards your consort, which was foreign to your nature. It was I who corrupted your heart—my insatiable vanity, which could not admit a partner in your affection, has ruined your character in the eyes of all good men; you, whom God designed to be a kind and considerate father of your daughter, are regarded as a wretch delighting to punish the supposed disobedience of your children."*

To you, dearest lady Anne, I bequeath

the power of making known the truth—
and when you do so, remind the queen,
that I shall then have rendered the fatal
account where eternal punishment awaits
the guilty! Implore her not to add one
curse to my lengthened misery . . . .
and, may the fact, that I shall have ceased
to exist when this reaches you, excite in
your bosom the spirit of forgiveness towards the memory of one, who, in her
varied passage through life, thought it a
high honour to subscribe herself your ladyship's friend.

The Countess of GUERNSEY.

*A correct copy of the letter alluded to in page 39,
and enclosed in the above packet.*

Philadelphia, August 10, 1807.

TO THE RIGHT HONOURABLE THE COUNTESS OF
GUERNSEY.

MADAM—As an independent man, and,
at this time, the resident of a free state, I
take the opportunity of declaring to your
ladyship, that I am the mysterious individual who lately lived near the mansion
of the injured princess of Wales; injured, I fear, by me, who knew only her
goodness, and her charities! Be pleased,
madam, to say to that lady, that I can
never cease to regret the having been, I
beg to say unintentionally, the cause of
one moment's uneasiness to her royal
highness by having in my possession a
miniature likeness of her royal highness.
Doubtless, the persons, who so far tres-
passed on the rights of society as to force
open my escrutoire, examined well its
contents; in which case they must have
seen the likenesses of each member of the

K 2

royal family of England. I was, therefore, at a loss to guess why the resemblance of the princess of Wales should have
given umbrage, whilst the others were
suffered to remain unnoticed—but, I have
been since informed, that her enemies
were seeking proofs of accusation against
the princess, and meant to adduce this as
one. I earnestly solicit your ladyship to
honour me with laying this letter before
the prince of Wales. I beg to assure his
royal highness that my person is wholly
unknown to the princess, and that my sole
occupation in England was the same which
caused my companions, *Francois* and *Lou-
is Meunier*, to be arrested at Worcester, in
the year 1793. I was, at that time, in
London, and, gaining caution from their
misfortune, I contrived, by various dis-
guises, to pursue the object of my unwea-
ried labour, free from suspicion, until the
late circumstance attracted public notice,
and compelled me from prudential motives,
having collected all the plans and sketches

it was my business to obtain, to sail with the first vessel from London to this place.

I entreat, at your ladyship's hand, to lose no time in communicating this intelligence to the prince and princess of Wales. I hope to have it in my power to be more explicit; but, for the present, the interests of France demand, that I only subscribe myself, with profound respect,

A Citizen of the American Republic.

The Queen's Last Letter to the King.

TO THE EDITOR.

Sir—Having read, with no uncommon interest, the "Confessions of the late Countess of Guernsey," and being acquainted with an important fact, hitherto concealed, as well as having in my possession A LETTER, written by her late majesty, but never received by the illustrious personage to whom it was addressed, I herewith enclose them for insertion, con-

ceiving yours to be decidedly the best
channel for them to obtain that publicity
which such a subject deserves. How I
came possessed of the documents in question, and the causes that have hitherto prevented their being published, will, I am
aware, be matter of curiosity to many; the
time, however, is not yet arrived, when
the disclosure of certain circumstances,
connected with this apparently mysterious
transaction, is either prudent or safe. You
are, therefore, at liberty to print them, or
return the packet, according to the address, as you may think most advisable;
and am, sir,

Yours, &c.

A. H.

The Real Cause of the Queen's Death stated.

It is generally supposed that her majesty received her death-blow in the conduct adopted towards her on the memorable 19th of July, 1821; doubtless, the in-

sults offered her, stung the queen deeply;
but she received a later and a more fatal
wound in her repulse at Carlton palace.
It will be remembered that, a short time
previous to her majesty's death, a female
was noticed about the precincts of that
mansion, who, when asked her business,
replied, she wished for an interview with
the king. The servants chid her intrusion,
and threatened the seizure of her person,
should she continue to trouble them. Her
majesty *(for it was the queen disguised)*
finding she was supposed to be a lunatic,
as a last effort, made an acknowledgment
to the sentinel that she was his queen, and
that her motive for seeking admission in
that disguise, was, to present a petition to
his royal master. The guard protested
he dared not solicit her admission. She
then requested he would himself be the
bearer of her letter to his gracious majes-
y: he promised to do so: but this he
merely did to satisfy her importunity, not
with an intention to fulfil his word, since

he knew an attempt of the kind would
draw upon him his dismissal from the
service. Intending, however, to act hon-
estly, he did the only thing in his power;
he took back the letter, which he gave to
her faithful servant, a foreigner, and he,
not well comprehending the matter, from
his ignorance of the English language,
said, when he returned it to his royal mistress, that " *a soldier had brought that from
the palace.*" The unfortunate lady, supposing her letter had been presented to the
king, and that he refused to look at it,
manifested greater poignancy of feeling
than she had done during her misfortunes.
On receiving the letter, her majesty placed
her hand on her heart, saying: " Here
ends my useless struggles:—*he is deceived,
and I must submit to the blow!* . . . .
The queen remained some time in her
chamber, taking, it was thought, repose;
but, on her re-appearance, her countenance indicated extreme mental suffering.
That same evening (as must be in the re-

collection of the public) her majesty visited Drury-lane theatre; but from that hour, her words and actions showed she had done with the world, and that hope and fear were equally at rest! Her wrongs formed a weighty mass, to which her thoughts naturally reverted, and she died as one to whom much was due, but whose charity forgave it all!

THE LETTER.

Brandenburgh House, July 29, 1821.

MY LIEGE AND HUSBAND!

Once more, and for the last time, I make my solemn appeal to your majesty for that justice which has hitherto been denied to me. My heart, torn with conflicting emotions, a prey to anguish and despair, would fain seek some repose from the troubles which have so long oppressed it, and pants for an opportunity to disburden itself of its load, before I descend into the silent grave. My gracious sovereign, I ask not for your love—I ask not even for your society. I wish to put no restraint upon your inclinations, nor to interfere with those pleasure which you feel indispensible to your happiness. Alas! too well I know that every artifice has been made use of to rivet the most unfavourable impressions in your breast, nor can I *now* even hope to see them wholly eradicated; but, oh! have pity on my unmerited sufferings, and, for once, at least, allow a hopeless and disconsolate wife to make known her griefs to the rightful, though estranged partner of her bosom. Shall the honour of my father's house be sullied, because his child could find no one to protect her from the malice of her traducers? Shall it indeed be said, that the monarch of a mighty empire—born to rule and to be beloved—a man, pre-eminently gifted with intellect and nobleness of soul—suffered his passions so far to outrun his reason, as to believe in the most monstrous fictions that the tongue of slander ever in-

vented?—False friends and open foes have
alike contributed towards my destruction.
A deep-laid system of deception has been
unceasingly practising on us both; and
too late, alas! have I discovered the, ma-
chinations of my enemies. It is this discovery alone that now prompts me to make
a last appeal to your royal breast. The
information I have lately obtained lays
open such a scene of depravity, such intrigues and perjuries, that I shudder, not
merely at the state to which they have re-
duced *me*, but to contemplate the extent
of human wickedness, and the dreadful
lengths to which the minions of a court
will go, to obtain their unhallowed de-
sires! Bred up under a tender mother's
eye, in my youth I knew no guile, and
therefore suspected none; my heart was
formed by nature for generous confidence
and sympathising love; unpractised in the
ways of deception myself, how could I
think there were beings base enough to
spread their snares, like spiders' webs, and

watch, with greedy eyes, for an opportunity of pouncing upon their prey?—Yet by
such, alas! was I beset as soon as I reached this boasted land of freedom; and before I even had an opportunity of making
myself acquainted with the ordinary cus-
toms of the country, the envenomed
tongue of slander was busy in _" filching
from me my good name." Little, indeed,
did I suppose that, in this generous land,
the *real* failings of a fellow-creature would
be propagated with avidity—how, then,
could I be prepared to defend myself from
unfounded calumnies! I had not then learnt
that,—

> " On eagles' wings immortal scandals fly,
> While virtuous actions are but born and die."

Little did I suspect that the fearlessness
of innocence would ever be construed into
unfeminine boldness; little did I imagine,
that charitable actions could not be performed without some secret, guilty motive being attributed to them; little did I
dream that I was doomed to be made the

sport of party, and have every action of my life publicly discussed, and praised or censured, as best suited the views and interests of opposite factions. How, then, could I a stranger and a female, guard against the poisoned shafts of calumny, when neither strength, dexterity, nor the most cautious prudence can enable a *man* to protect himself, if so assailed? Had I *known* my secret enemies, perhaps I might have avoided them, and exposed their wiles; but I was surrounded and flattered by them, and taught to confide in them as my most devoted friends!

It was my peculiar misfortune to form a wrong estimate of the necessary qualifications for a female of distinguished rank to possess; had I exchanged my natural candour, openness, and love of innocent pastimes, for formal reserve, courtly etiquette, and dissimulation, those actions, which resulted from an exuberance of sensibility, would never have appeared; and the malignant would have had no opportunity of torturing them into what they first termed *levities*, but which afterwards assumed the appellation of *indiscretions;* and at length were called *criminal indulgences!*—till I was in the end denounced as a traitor to my sovereign, and faithless to my husband's bed!

Great, however, as my wrongs are; mercilessly as I have been persecuted; held up as I still am for the finger of scorn to point at, I forbear to recriminate; and would be content, were merely my own happiness concerned, to quit this world of sorrow without giving utterance to one word of reproach, gladly consigning the recollection of all my injuries to oblivion. But, oh, my husband! when I reflect on the depth of misery in which I have been plunged, and contrast it with the innocent enjoyments of my youth, or the high expectations I formed of happiness in becoming the wife of an enlightened and accomplished prince—when my mind reverts to that distressing moment, when the

dear child of my bosom was unfeelingly
torn from a mother's arms—when I look
back at the many foul attempts which
were made to rob me of my honour and
stab my peace of mind, till, dreading a foe
in every countenance, I fled the country
where I ought to have found friends and
protectors, and sought an asylum among
strangers—when, although seas divided
me from my persecutors, their rancorous
hate pursued me, and, encompassed by
spies, I was hunted and ensnared even in
my exile—when the last hope of a disconsolate mother was bereft me, and I bowed
to the dispensations of Providence in the
loss of HER, whose life and happiness was
far dearer to me than my own—when foreign courts were base enough to join the
ranks of my enemies, and treat a defence-
less and unoffending woman with every
species of indignity—when the prayers of
the church were denied me, and the un-
derlings of power blasphemously declared,
that the altar should not be polluted with

the name of their queen—oh! when all
these horrible and heart-rending recollec-
tions press on my mind, that spirit of fortitude, which has hitherto sustained me,
sinks under the mighty load; my blood
runs cold with horror; and I feel that *the*
hour fast approaches when death must
close my eyes, and put a period to my
earthly sufferings.

My gracious sovereign! it is the guilty
mind alone that can dread the approach
of the last hour. The martyr in a righteous cause smiles at the engines of torture,
and joyfully hails the moment that frees
him from his persecutors; yet, with his
dying lips, he prays to the throne of mercy, and, as he expires, imitates the language of HIM who died to atone for our
transgressions; "Father! forgive them,
for they know not what they do." Yes,
indeed, I feel that I can quit the scene of
such countless wo without regret—nay,
with calm tranquillity and delight; and, as
regards myself,

" Cast not one longing, lingering look behind."

And when my soul takes her flight to the mansions of eternal bliss, I shall fervently pray, that mercy may be extended to those who knew not how to show mercy to me. For

" Of all the paths which lead to human bliss,
The most secure and grateful to our steps
With mercy and humanity is marked.—
And how much brighter is the wreath of glory,
When interwove with clemency and justice?"

I am not insensible of the value of the good opinion of the world; and far be it from me to despise the public voice, or to disregard the general feeling; but I scorn hypocrisy, and have no desire to be thought better than I am; nor would I, even now, humbled and degraded as I may appear in the estimation of my enemies, do an act derogatory to truth, honour, and justice, were it possible that by so doing I should gain the wealth of an empire, or be put in possession of those rights which I have so urgently, but fruitlessly, demanded at your hands!

Alas! alas! how can I hope to make known to you the secret cause of our mutual troubles, if an interview be not granted? how can I expect to convince *you*, who have so often shown that you are not open to conviction? Yet, with the proofs I now possess, I should do even your majesty an injustice, were I not to attempt to disclose those facts, which no other human being will ever dare to disclose. *My* mind is at peace with all the world, and nothing that can now happen can possibly destroy my inward serenity. Allow me, then, the gratification of pouring the balm of consolation (for *some* consolation *I can administer*) into that bosom, which, at times, must be a prey to anguish!

Should, however, my prayers and intreaties prove of no avail—should insult be added to . . . . ; and fresh calumnies be heaped on my guiltless head,—oh, may I still preserve my reason, and, with christian resignation learn to submit with patience to my fate! I have no selfish views

to gratify; no ambitious motives stimulate
my actions:—my whole life bears evidence, that neither pride nor vain-glory
lurks within me; but I have a tender regard for the honour of the house of Brunswick, and with my latest breath shall I
declare, that I never sullied that honour,
so gloriously maintained by the blood of
my dearest kindred! And will it then be
credited, that I could stoop to degrade
the noble and generous English? (for they
have, in spite of power and oppression,
voluntarily testified their love for me.)
Can it be believed, that a queen, who saw
she reigned in the hearts of her people,
would, by her own act, forfeit their good
opinion of her? Can the most sceptical of
the human race (not previously bent on my
destruction) in their conscience *believe,*
that, if guilty of the crimes laid to my
charge, I would rush, at the peril of my
life, to confront my accusers, and that, too,
at a time when my degradation was the
high road to favour?—Such a doctrine is

irreconcileable with common sense, and repugnant to human feelings.

And here allow me, my liege, to pay that grateful homage, which I so truly feel, to the great bulk of the British nation; nor think that, when I thus commemorate their generosity and attachment, I mean any disrespect to their sovereign. The people of England are, indeed, a loyal people; and their generous ardour in endeavouring to rescue a female from oppression, is perfectly consistent with the most exalted notions of loyalty and chivalric honour. May your majesty long reign in their hearts, and may the state be guided by such counsels as shall best contribute to its welfare, and the happiness of those over whom you reign!

I shall pass over with a sigh the cruel repulse I met with on that gorgeous day, which saw you crowned, because my wish is not to cast the slightest reproach; but I feel it is a sacred duty, before I lay down my pen, to declare, that in that act I was guided by no advice opposite to my own inclinations; and it equally behoves me to declare, that, although I hold in the highest estimation the opinions of those devoted friends who have adhered to their persecuted queen, " through evil report and through good report," yet I have acted all along agreeable to the dictates of my own heart, and am alone accountable for every step I have taken. Should this letter, contrary to my expectation, ever be seen by the public, it will doubtless meet with the animadversions of those enemies, whom nothing short of my death will satisfy; for I have long since found, that, to such malignant beings, were my conduct proved to be

> " Chaste as the icicle
> That's curdled by the frost from purest snow,"

still they would discover spots of the deadliest hue, and strive, with renewed virulence, to blacken my reputation. But, although they neither feel compunction for

the injuries they have done me, nor pity
for my woes, I freely forgive them; well
knowing that a day of retribution must
overtake them; and that, however they
may now triumph over my misfortunes,
they cannot deprive me of my integrity
and innocence, nor interpose between me
and the righteous judge of heaven!

CAROLINE R.

THE END.

CPSIA information can be obtained
at www.ICGtesting.com
Printed in the USA
BVOW06s2017160117
473628BV00013B/215/P